ANIMALS

GORILLAS

by Mary Ellen Klukow

AMICUS | AMICUS INK

face

hand

Look for these
words and pictures
as you read.

back

nest

Look! What is moving through the forest? It is a gorilla!

Gorillas live in troops.
A troop is a family group.

face

Look at the face.
It looks like yours.
Gorillas are related to people.

hand

Look at the hand.
It has a thumb.
It grabs plants to eat. Yum!

Look at his back.
The old males have silver hair.
They are in charge.

back

Look at the nest.
She makes a new one every day.
She sleeps in it.

nest

Baby gorillas sleep with their mom.
Soon they will build their own nest.

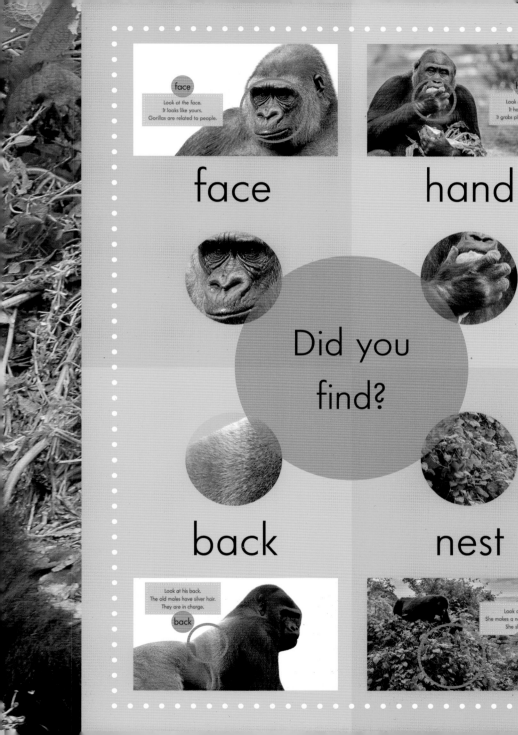

face

Look at the face.
It looks like yours.
Gorillas are related to people.

hand

Look at the hand.
It has a thumb.
It grabs plants to eat. Yum!

Did you find?

back

Look at his back.
The old males have silver hair.
They are in charge.

nest

Look at the nest.
She makes a new one every day.
She sleeps in it.

spot

Spot is published by Amicus and Amicus Ink
P.O. Box 1329, Mankato, MN 56002
www.amicuspublishing.us

Library of Congress Cataloging-in-Publication Data
Names: Klukow, Mary Ellen, author.
Title: Gorillas / by Mary Ellen Klukow.
Description: Mankato, Minnesota : Amicus, [2020] | Series:
  Spot. African animals | Audience: K to Grade 3. |
Identifiers: LCCN 2018025817 (print) | LCCN 2018031232
  (ebook) | ISBN 9781681517223 (pdf) | ISBN
  9781681516400 (library binding) | ISBN 9781681524269
  (paperback) | ISBN 9781681517223 (ebook)
Subjects: LCSH: Gorilla--Africa--Juvenile literature.
Classification: LCC QL737.P94 (ebook) | LCC QL737.P94
  K58 2020 (print) | DDC 599.884--dc23
LC record available at https://lccn.loc.gov/2018025817

Printed in China

HC 10 9 8 7 6 5 4 3 2 1
PB 10 9 8 7 6 5 4 3 2 1

Wendy Dieker and Alissa Thielges, editors
Deb Miner, series designer
Ciara Beitlich, book designer
Holly Young, photo researcher

Photos by Shutterstock/Nick Fox
cover, 16; iStock/GlobalP 1; iStock/
ANDREYGUDKOV 3; Alamy/Terry
Whittaker 4–5; 123RF/anolis01 6–7;
Getty miroslav_1 8–9; Shutterstock/
Chad Littlejohn 10–11; Biosphoto/Robert
Haasmann/imageBROKER 12–13; iStock/
Jaroslav3355 14

GORILLAS